Not My Circus, Not My Monkeys

100 poems for today's crazy world...plus an interview with the author

OREST STOCCO

Not My Circus, Not My Monkeys

Copyright © 2017 by OREST STOCCO

All rights reserved. No part of this book may be reproduced or transmitted in any form or by any means without written permission of the author.

ISBN 978-1-926442-18-1

Edited by Penny Lynn Cates
Cover Design by Penny Lynn Cates

"Not my circus, not my monkeys."

—*Polish Proverb*

"Many pioneers can tell a story of misery,
all due to the primitive misoneism
of their contemporaries."

THE UNDISCOVERED SELF
—*C. G. Jung*

CONTENTS

What the Hell Is Going On Out There?.. 1
Interview with a Shaman.. 2
Life.. 3
Mary, Mary, Mary.. 4
Birth of a Mystic.. 5
Silver Lining.. 6
The Thirtieth Bird.. 7
Wasteland of Misery.. 9
Tough Love.. 10
God Within.. 11
Out of the Ashes.. 12
Mount Ulysses... 13
On the Menu Today... 14
My Struggle... 15
Alchemy of the Self... 16
The Bet... 17
Birds of a Feather.. 18
The In-between Days... 19
The Prize.. 20
New Pastures..21
I Am Where I Want to Be..22
Self-Murder..23
Lunch with a Friend...24
The Coiled Serpent of My Soul...26
Weasel Words..27
Poets and Artists... 28
A Weird Dream..29
Mothering Instinct... 30
The Old Fox... 31
The Soul of a Liar..32
Memories of My Mother..33
My Journal...34
That's Poetry..36
The Old Gadfly's Mission..37

An Old French Proverb	38
Dinosaur Man	39
The Poet's Mystique	40
Bob and Carol	41
My Stolen Book	43
Master of Broken Boundaries	45
The Road Taken	47
Conundrum	48
The Devil's Shadow	49
Memories of Her Past Life	50
A Stain Upon His Soul	52
The Forbidden Teaching	53
The Poet and His English Teacher	54
Time Traveler	55
Every Poet Is a Joyce	56
Doors	57
Homo Nuovo	58
The Writer's Heart	59
A Window	61
The Poet's Daemon	62
Envy	63
Cycles of Life	64
Redemption	65
Meaning	66
Cancer of the Soul	67
My Legacy	68
Lunch at Moxie's	69
Mending the Circle	70
Sensory Pleasure	71
Pinning the Devil Down	72
Dogs of Desire	73
Master Assemblers	75
The Housefly	76
Somerset Maugham	77

No More!	78
Distress	79
Mixed Feelings	80
Lifeblood	81
There Is One Sin	82
The Smell of Life	83
Efficiency	84
A Writer's Lament	85
The Letter	86
Harvard Boy	87
Stairway of Heaven	88
Making Music	89
Philosopher's Stone	90
New Age Religion	91
Karma	92
Specter of the Project	93
Jehovah's Witnesses at My Door	94
The Messenger	95
Ode to the Poet	96
By Their Voice We Know Them	97
Child Brody	98
Smoothies	99
Biography of a Lesbian Poet	100
The Making of an Atheist	101
Duende	102
Bad News	103
The Stuff of Life	104
My Quandary for the Day	105
Peach Cobbler	106
A Sacred Contract	107
Tribute to Emily	108
The Circus Never Stops	109
Interview with the Author	110

What the Hell Is Going On Out There?

Hierophants of the world,
what the hell is going on out there?
Your antennae are out of whack,
and all you report is madness,
madness, and more madness, or
am I too blind to see?

Hierophants of the world,
tell me the truth, has the world
gone mad or is this some new sanity
beyond my ability to process
and understand?

Hierophants of the world,
I've lost all faith in religion, science,
and politics, but not in the better nature
of my fellow man, so please tell me:
what the hell is going on out there?

Interview with a Shaman

"Only ignorance
denies these things,"
said the shaman to the head
on the pole;
"I don't need to believe,
I know."

The path was difficult,
far away and deep, and
his guide a winged fantasy;
but archival wisdom and
serendipity saved the day,
and sanity prevailed.

"But surely, death is an end?"
the head on the pole refrained;
but with a twinkle in his eye,
the shaman replied: "Yes,
it is an end. "And there we
are not quite certain."

And so it went...

Life

I

The pressure is off,
the path is no more;
the dandelion and the rose
breathe the same air, and
the path begins anew.

II

Ten thousand acorns
fell from the oak,
five took root
and one became
a tree.

Mary, Mary, Mary

There's a line you cannot cross,
not for want of crossing it,
you dare not! — and the sacred mystery
remains sacred, all the food you crave
to feed your famished soul.

They flock to you like errant flies,
in the misery of their broken lives,
comforted by your sapient words because
they have no words of their own.

"I don't know what a soul is, or even if
we have one." — *So profound, so profound!*
And the merry-go-round goes around
and around the sacred mystery
of your famished soul.

Birth of a Mystic

She did not want to,
she had to! —
the way was too steep
for the great unwashed,
and her *daemon*
pleaded, —

"Tease them, tease them!"

But the more she teased
them, the more they needed
what she could not give
them, —

Sorely, she dropped hints
and clues aplenty, but still
the world puzzled; —

And when she died,
oh so weary, oh so weary,
leaving a trail like Ariadne,
the world conceded
and the poet became
a mystic.

Silver Lining

The longest journey
is the shortest way
when you don't know
how to get there.
Why me, God? you shout,
and storm away in anger.
And then you die the little
death and thank God
for your suffering, and
you go the rest of the way
joyful in your blessing.

The Thirtieth Bird

I sipped my coffee, pondering,
wondering, wondering, wondering,
when all I really had to do
was to just wait and see.

Like a bird lighting on a tree,
an idea always comes to me;
and I gratefully study
the new bird in my tree.

A bird lighted this morning,
a bird I knew too well,
but the emotions it awakened
overcame me.

It takes grit and sensitivity
to tell this bird's story,
but few poets have the courage
to bare their soul this way.

A million birds of every feather
went on a quest for their Creator;
only thirty completed the journey,
and looked into the Face of God.

The Face that these rare birds saw
was not what they expected,
and they rested and grew strong
in their great realization.

I took another sip of coffee,
and one more for good measure;
but before I could steel my courage,
my bird had flown away.

Wasteland of Misery

I'm stuck in a crack
between this world and that,
and I fear stepping into my life.
This happens every now and then
when I have things I don't want to do,
and the longer I put them off the wider
the crack gets. I used to fool myself by
replacing one responsibility with another,
but the crack only got wider; and now I
bite the bullet and suffer the conflict
of **not doing what I have to do and just
going out and doing it**, and I pine my
life away in a wasteland of misery.

Tough Love

"Stop cheating,"
said her grandmother,
for the third or fourth time,
but Kelly May, who loved to win,
reacted like a spoiled child,
"Then I'm going to play by myself
and cheat all I want!" Three weeks
later, Kelly May called her grandmother,
bawling on the phone, "Grandma, the
cat ate my bird," and grandma replied,
"Tough luck kid, that's life."

God Within

Flat, existential plane
of life and limb,
toiling, toiling, toiling
for profit unseen.
One day a voice speaks
from within:
"Go to the casino,"
and all the profit
that you win
goes to life and limb,
and the voice confirms
God within.

Out of the Ashes

The nastiest,
beastliest purgation
striking from God knows where,
combustible spark, cigarette butt,
lightning bolt from heaven—
eighty-eight thousand souls
displaced from safe haven,
forfeiting happy gain—
God knows when the purging will end
and life reclaimed from the ashes
of their weary soul, but the spirit of wild
rose country cannot be broken, and
the Phoenix will rise again.

Mount Ulysses

Sunday, May 8, 2016, 8:51 A. M.
Mother's Day, Penny hoisted her
book into the air and declared,
"Yea! Done!" That was her reaction
to the greatest novel of the 20th Century,
Ulysses, by James Joyce, and when
asked what she thought of it,
she reflected, and said,
"Yea! Done!"

On the Menu Today

Coincidence or editorial play, I do not know,
three articles side by side in my *Sunday Star*;
in the middle, wedged in like a freshly dug grave,
90-year-old retired senator and his 40-year-old
male lover, 15-year affair now marital bliss. The
senator was married before to his great love
of 38 years, their children older than his lover
who filled the hole in his life when his wife died
of acute leukemia, the second great love of his
nonagenarian life; to the left of Harris and Matthew
an article on the Freegan Pony restaurant in Paris,
meals prepared from dumpster food from Rungis
international food market, and to the right of
Matthew and Harris an article on *Laab dib,*
a northern Thai specialty of raw blood, bile,
and herbs, an acquired taste—
"a meal to die for."

My Struggle

"What emerged from this
was myself," wrote the voluble
author of *My Struggle*. "This was
what was me." But how many pages
did it take the Norwegian writer to
see himself as his life had shaped him?
I know the story well. Book after book
after book my struggle told itself, but
never in full; until one day, I don't
know when, Old Whore Life
showed her face to me, and
I saw that she was me!

Alchemy of the Self

The agony of my life was being
a stranger to myself, because the
person who was me was not the
person I wanted to be; so I broke
the mirror of my life and suffered
the pain of putting myself together
again into the person I was meant
to be; and now I no longer suffer
the agony of being a stranger to
myself, because I *am* me.

The Bet

I made a bet on the Other Side
that I would find my way out of life
with nothing but my wit, no mentor,
guru, or philosophy to guide me
through the maze of human misery,
forging my own path through life
on the anvil of my blemished soul,
a man in every way the same as other
men but with one distinction: an
unparalleled desire to absolve myself
of my regretful life which I returned
to live over again to achieve a different
outcome, and I can't wait to pass over
to the Other Side to claim my bet from
the soul of a man called Pythagoras,
who was once my teacher.

Birds of a Feather

Every moment of every day, year after year after year
they gather from every corner of the world—large
and small, fat and thin, black and white, brown
and yellow, and every shade in-between the races,
and plan their journey to the magical kingdom
of their deepest longing.

I gathered one day, seventeen years, five months, two days,
five hours, ten minutes, and seven seconds to the moment
when I read *The Razor's Edge* that called me to the gathering;
silently, pulling me through the rutted corridors of my life
despite bitter protestations, and I began my lonely journey
to the magical kingdom of my deepest longing.

All of us strangers with the same desire, we embarked upon
our separate ways, alone and frightened to the bone; and every
now and then we met along the way and compared our progress:
O, what dismay! O, what catastrophe! O, what simple joy!
And we continued with newfound wisdom, only to lose
our way again in life's brambles; but I persisted—

And strewn along the byways of life, countless birds of a feather
torn to shreds on the razor's edge and beaten to dejection; but
I persevered, fearing to fail as I had done the last time I gathered
in the wild frontier of the new land of the Americas— Lord
Daniel Wellington, aka trapper Dan, who drowned in vain
trying to gain the kingdom of my deepest longing.

The In-between Days

37 years old, much too young
to face the dreaded divide
with nothing but naked fear
and wanton desire for the time
she had left to live, with little
thought of the Other Side—
absolute nullification of her
selfhood and vague rumors
passed on from generations of
desperate hope—and like a
fierce tornado of unlived dreams
she sucked the sweet marrow
out of life to satisfy her craving
for personal meaning, keeping
a memoir for posterity of the
in-between days of her vital
treatments: 137 soul-drenched
pages of precious living.

The Prize

If life is a game,
then what's the prize?
"The prize is to open your eyes,"
said my partner Penny Lynn,
playfully. "And see what?" I replied.
But that's the mystery of the game
of life that we all get caught up in,
by whatever name we call it,
like actress/director Jodie Foster
and her new game of *Money Monster*;
and not until we see the hole in our
soul will our eyes be wide open.
And then we stare wide-eyed and ask
the dreaded question: "Now what?"
And the game of life is taken to new
levels of authenticity: "Beauty is truth,
truth beauty," and we stop playing
the game of make-believe and
start living life for real.

New Pastures

The valley no longer beckons,
and she ascends again sans the burden
of old thoughts. No more demands upon
unwary souls as they graze on earthly longings;
and when the luscious grass has been eaten,
they climb to news pastures where she
will be waiting with new poems
for them to graze on.

I Am Where I Want to Be

No more questing in the dry pages
of lost horizons, or climbing mountains
in the Hindu Kush searching for a fantasy;
and no more meditating in walled Tibetan caves
or collecting wild honey like a mendicant Sufi,
because I am where I want to be.

I could be sunning on a sandy beach in Florida,
cycling in Provence, or sipping espresso in Tuscany,
exploring new writers for new thoughts and taking
up hiking or hobbies like Tai Chi and Mediterranean
cooking, but life no longer beckons me because
I am where I want to be.

Not every acorn that falls off the oak will grow
into its own tree, only the seeds that take root will
become what they are encoded to be; so it is with
every soul that takes root in the humble soil of
its own garden, growing where it has been
planted to become what it's meant to be.

Self-Murder

The lady was in tears:
she could not negate
the self she had become
trying desperately to undo
millions of years of evolution,
to her Master's indifference
who responded with a coldness
that made my blood boil.
"Try harder," said the Master,
but the harder the lady tried
to negate her own identity,
the more her soul resisted;
and in despair, she overdosed
on sleeping pills to become
one with Non-Being just
to please her Master
of Nothingness.

Lunch with a Friend

I stopped in just to say hello to my friend
and neighbor who had come up from Toronto
to his cozy cottage in Georgian Bay that he
had built with his own hands. Born in Calabria
where I came from with my family when I
was five, Tony and I made wine together last
summer and shared it over the winter and
spring, and we'll be making wine again in
the new season, and when I dropped in from
my bike ride he was roasting some lamb on
his barbeque, along with mushrooms and
red peppers, and he invited me to lunch with
him and Maria whose husband died of cancer
a few years ago. My friend's wife dropped
dead of a heart attack while building the cottage,
and after five or six years of a bad relationship
with a Sicilian widow who couldn't control her
drinking, he met Maria at a wedding reception
for a mutual Italian acquaintance, and now
they live together for companionship as many
widows often do, which took their children
time to get used to; and with each passing year
they grow more intimate and respectful of each
other's quirks and habits and even laugh at
them now in front of me. Lunch was a simple
feast of love of food and sharing, an Italian
custom like no other, and I had to politely stop
Maria four or five times from over-serving me,
reminding her of my mother saying to guests

at our family table, *"Manga, manga."* I loved
the freshly-picked asparagus risotto with the
barbequed lamb, large-capped mushrooms,
and long red peppers, and the simple lettuce
salad with salt and pepper and oil and vinegar
dressing, and crusty Calabrese bread just like
my mother used to make every Wednesday
morning to soak up all the juices from my plate,
and a glass of red wine to toast our lunch and
friendship; and, what I really enjoyed because
Penny and I don't drink it at home, a tiny cup
of espresso coffee with a drop of Anisette and
a tiny spoonful of sugar, and after lunch Tony
and I sat in his garage with the door wide open
soaking up the spring sun and talking, I mostly
listening to his life story, wishing that my father
had been as adaptive and resourceful, and I
couldn't have asked for a nicer neighbor in
our new home in Georgian Bay.

The Coiled Serpent of My Soul

I didn't plan it, nor could I have done so:
when the time is right life gives birth to new
meaning in the experience, and writing my last
inspired musing took me by surprise; not that
I wanted it to be my last, they had served the
purpose they were born to serve and the coiled
serpent of my soul sprung with such surprise that
I was awash in a soothing balm of calm—no more
demands to feed the hungry beast that turned its
nose at the banquet table of sacred purpose, no
more waiting for the divine bird to light upon the
branches of my mind; just the resolve that it was
time to move on to another path to serve the soul
of the great unwashed: poetry, stories, and novels
to warm the cold beast's heart, and one wonders
why the secret is kept secret from the masses
that want the truth but can't bear it when
it is served to them on a platter.

Weasel Words

It's not the word you have to blame,
by calling it a weasel; the poor creature
did no harm. He sucks the meat out
of the egg to honor its instinct for
survival and is true to its own nature;
but man—*o, what a paradox he is!* —
who is both what he is and what he is
not, and when he sucks the meat out
of words to have his cake and eat it too,
it's not the word that is to blame by
calling it a weasel, but the man
for his deception.

Poets and Artists

There are no shortcuts to salvation,
because there is nothing to be saved from;
we are born to become what we're meant
to be, and we will all get there eventually.
It will take more than one lifetime, to be
sure; but what does it matter in the end
if time is never-ending? But we don't know
that, do we? And we look for shortcuts to
salvation because we can't wait to get
there. We practice the Five Tibetan Rites
for eternal youth, and meditate for cosmic
awareness, garden until our hearts overflow,
and run marathons until we're a hundred;
but in the end we're the same soul as when
we started, only a little wiser, and we wonder
what all the fuss was about. Everything
matters, and nothing matters; it all depends
upon where we stand. But all the same we
have to live, and making choices is our
nature; that's the game we have to play,
because we don't know any better. Some
play it fair, and some don't; but fair or not
it's still a game, and every winner becomes
a loser and every loser a winner, but we all
become a little wiser. And we play and play
and play, and when we're wise enough
we come back as poets and artists.

A Weird Dream

I had a weird dream last night.
I was happy and resolved, the man
I spent years of conscious labor giving
birth to, exercising my privilege to
become what Mother Nature could
not finish, but the woman I was with
could not fathom the mystery of my
nature and got pregnant by another
man, a handsome and talented hockey
player still in the throes of Mother
Nature (he was an abusive alcoholic);
and then my dream changed, and I
saw three suspicious men planning to
assassinate the President of Mexico
and I had to forewarn him of the plot,
and then I woke up wondering what
C. G. Jung, who analyzed more than
80,000 dreams in his long career and
called dreams "the guiding words of
the soul," would have made of it.

Mothering Instinct

She could not have children
of her own, but her mothering
instinct came out today when she
brought two baby birds fallen from
their nest home to look after, but
one baby bird was badly wounded
and didn't respond to her loving
care, and the other pined for its
own mother. We put the baby birds
back into the box she had brought
them in and drove back to where
she had found them under the tree
where they had fallen for their
own mother to take care of them.

The Old Fox

He was right after all, the Old Fox,
pushing all their buttons to bring out
their chief feature, the darkest secret
of their nature, and they only stayed
with him who rose to the occasion
and put their need for greater meaning
above ephemeral self-interest. No-one
knew where he came from, he kept
that secret to make his teaching more
alluring, and they hung upon his every
word until they could take no more,
and they left more broken than when
they came, writing books and maligning
his intention; but the Old Fox knew
what he was doing, feeding the hungry
and starving the poor, and those that
stayed to hear the worst went away
wiser in the sacred knowledge of their
chief feature that blinded them to
their true nature.

The Soul of a Liar

It's not true, what they say about you,
it's a lie like all the other lies that they say
about everybody they talk about, because
nothing they say can be trusted, —

Why is that?

They mean well, but they continue to lie
despite their good intentions, and they
never stop lying even when they
know they are lying, —

Why is that?

They lie best when they tell the truth,
which is the mystery of the liar's nature,
and not until they can no longer suffer
who they are will they stop lying, —

Why is that?

Memories of My Mother

Another one of life's ironic moments—
    my curmudgeon neighbor across the street
with his long-handled dandelion weeder
    hunched over like an ogre on the hunt for
the pesky yellow flower, and me on my front deck
    reading in my Saturday's *Globe & Mail* "What
you can do to help bees," featuring the new attitude
    adopted by Hog Town, Toronto the Good now
dubbed "Bee City," urging Torontonians to convert
    their lawns into habitats for pollinators, rallying a
cry to all city gardeners to forget the pesticides
    and let the dandelions sprout. I put my paper down
and stared at my snowbird neighbor in his baggy
    shorts and loose-fitting Florida shirt ogre away
on our resplendent spring flower, summoning long
    forgotten memories of my mother hunched over
in our yard and neighbor's lawn with an old kitchen
    knife and brown paper bag gathering fresh dandelion
leaves which she would rinse and sauté with olive
    oil and garlic for our dinner, but which I liked best
in a thick sandwich with mom's freshly-baked
    crusty Calabrese bread.

My Journal

Where do you go when you need comfort?
To your partner, mother, father, brother, sister, or good
friend who will listen to your woes and offer you kindness
and understanding; and if you have no-one to turn to,
what do you do?

Life never runs smoothly. We would like it to,
but on the whole life is all about transitions; and when
we're lulled into believing that life is going smoothly, out
of nowhere we're hit with a new transition, and we're
off to the races again.

That's what happened to me yesterday, picking up branches
and twigs from our yard from our long winter's passing,
my heart just wasn't up to the task and I exhausted myself
much more quickly than I expected; so I sat on my deck
to catch my breath, full of apprehension.

I so miss the use of my body, the never-ending stamina
that kept me going from morning till night, and I so miss
my long distance running that turned rotten days into
good ones; it's just a memory now, but what a glorious
memory, and I thank God for my endeavor.

I'm aware of life's transitions, and I never fight the march
of time—that's foolish madness; but all the same, it's nice
to have someone to talk to when the hammer comes crashing
down; that's why I turned to my journal this morning
and poured my heart out for a little comfort.

My journal is my best friend, always there to hear what I have to say; and, at the risk of revealing a secret, my journal always talks back to me. The voice that speaks is not my own—I know my own voice, surely; and as I pour my heart out, my journal always comforts me just by listening.

That's Poetry

I picked up Keats this morning,
    and then Shelley, but I wasn't in the mood
for either; and I picked up *Immortal Poems*
    of the English Language, but I decided to
make coffee instead; and as I waited for
    my coffee I browsed through a word book:
30 Days to a More Powerful Vocabulary—
    the more words we have, the better we can
express ourselves, indispensable for a poet;
    but my heart wasn't in it. I poured my coffee
and took a sip and pondered my situation:
    words, words, and more words. Knowledge,
knowledge, and more knowledge, and *"to the
    making of many books there is no end and
much study is a weariness of the flesh"* said the
    Preacher in *Ecclesiastes,* and we're back to
where we started. I opened my book on the
    immortal poems and read Shelly's *Ozymandias*
to give clarity to my feelings: it's not how
    many words we know, it's how we put
them together. That's poetry.

The Old Gadfly's Mission

The Old Gadfly of Athens had an Oracle,
    the sign of a voice that he called divine,
and it came to him when he was a child
    to tell him what not to do. It never told
him what to do, because he had free will;
    his Oracle spoke to him only when he
strayed too far from his mission to free
    soul from its prison. I, too, have an Oracle
that speaks to me; but it never tells me
    what to do or not to do because my Oracle
is my own free will; and the more I exercise
    my free will, the more my Oracle speaks
to me. But when I get myself into a pickle,
    I curse the gods like an errant boy and
get myself on track again to bring more
    clarity to the Old Gadfly's mission
of freeing soul from its prison.

An Old French Proverb

FREQUENCY is the world's new TEACHING,
And INTUITION our new teacher; no more
willful intention to manifest desire with
the Law of Attraction—yesterday's guarded
secret; ATTENTION will suffice to materialize
desire into being. And if our world suddenly
falls apart, we can piece it together better
than ever with a higher vibration; but raising
our frequency is the new mystery, and when
everything is said and done the new TEACHING
is no different from the old, the same wine in
a new bottle. As the French are fond of saying,
"Plus ça change, plus c'est la même chose."

Dinosaur Man

Dinosaur Man is dying,
not of disease or hunger,
but of fear of letting go
of his dinosaur body;
and as he gasps for air
he screams in anger and
rallies his strength to
stay alive. But Dinosaur
Man cannot stop the flow
of time, which is a cosmic
function, and as his body
quickens with the higher
frequency of service to life
and not himself he fights
to hold onto his power;
but time speeds on, and
one day, hopefully sooner
than later, Dinosaur Man
will be an artifact.

The Poet's Mystique

What does the poet know
that the rest of the world
doesn't?

Why does the world flock
to poets for the right
sentiment?

And why are poets
so difficult to understand
until we probe them?

Not everyone loves poetry,
but those that do cannot
get enough of it, —

Why is that?

Bob and Carol

They made a truce again
to not argue the whole day;
but the more wine they drank,
the more contentious
they became.

My mother made fried patties
with left-over mashed potatoes,
which I loved dearly, and I made
fried patties with left-over rice
and mashed potatoes too.

The evening was getting on,
and the wine was running low,
so Penny went into the house
and got more wine and a plate
of my rice and potato patties.

Bob and Carol are long retired,
and look for things to do;
Carol goes out shopping every day,
and Bob stays home and fiddles
about with little projects.

Couples argue for no apparent reason
other than to be right in their opinion,
and the more Bob and Carol drank
the more contentious they became

over my fried patties.

"They're made with mashed potatoes,"
contended Bob, who was born to be right;
and to hold onto her precious ground
Carol downed her wine and countered,
"They're made with cooked rice."

They broke their truce again that day,
as they fought for their opinion;
and when I told them that my patties
were made with left-over risotto rice
and mashed potatoes, they failed
to see the irony.

My Stolen Book

GREAT SHORT STORIES FROM THE WORLD'S LITERATURE, and stamped inside the front cover of the book: *Property of Nipigon Red Rock District High School*, which I stole five decades ago.

I love books, and I never tire of collecting them, especially books on great literature, my favorite passion; but I failed to see why I was so possessive of the books I gathered like a greedy hoarder.

Penny finished reading the book she had picked up on her weekend getaway to New York City with her two sisters, REPORT FROM GROUND ZERO, and she went through my library and selected the book I stole in grade twelve for her next read.

"These are the best of the best," I said to her, with a strange feeling of nostalgia; but when I went back to work on my new poem, I felt a storm brewing inside me. Not knowing what it was, I poured this feeling into "Bob and Carol" and ensouled my poem with its own mystery—the gnostic secret of great literature.

Penny read the first two stories this morning, "The Passover Guest" by Sholom Aleichem, and "A Passion in the Desert" by Honore De Balzac, and she enjoyed them as much as she enjoyed Alice Munro that I had introduced her to when she won the Nobel Prize for

Literature in 2013, and this didn't surprise me.

But a weird feeling came over me when she showed me the duct-taped copy of my stolen book this morning, and as I walked down the stairs for my second cup of coffee it hit me why it bothered me for her to read GREAT SHORT STORIES FROM THE WORLD'S LITERATURE.

It wasn't my stolen book that I fetished, nor the enviable artistry of the great short stories, but their hidden treasure; and the idea of her reading my stolen book threatened me, not for the precious life wisdom of the stories, but for my fear of her discovering in them my most coveted secret which I spent a lifetime ferreting out like a blind mole in the soul of the world's great literature.

Master of Broken Boundaries

Surfing the channels on TV one night I saw
the title *Another Woman,* which I had seen
before; but I was so intrigued the first time
that I decided to watch it once more.

I hate Woody Allen, who has mastered the
art of broken boundaries; but he wrote
and directed *Another Woman,* and I have
nothing but respect for his artistry.

It's not so much his cloying angst, which grows
more peevish with every new movie that he
makes, that exasperates me; but his seductive
sense of unbounded willful selfishness.

"The heart wants what the heart wants," Allen
justifies his personal ethics, which he projects
upon the screen of life, and he quotes Nietzsche
and Jean Paul Sartre to support him.

Jena Rowlands is the other woman in the move
Another Woman, reflecting Allen's recurring theme
of broken boundaries, and the story breaks when
Rowlands sees her stupefying self-deception.

But that's the secret of Woody Allen's longevity,
his wanton exploitation of man's vulnerable nature;
and not until this peevish little man respects moral
boundaries will I ever stop hating him.

The Road Taken

Sitting on my front deck in beautiful Georgian
Bay reading a book of immortal English poems
and listening to the sounds of nature, birds
chirping in the trees and splashing in the
bird bath and garrulous cement trucks down
the street pouring forms for our new neighbors
home, Lionel and Patricia, and Robert Frost
chanting, "The woods are lovely, dark, and deep
/But I have promises to keep /And miles to go
before I sleep," I smile in happy thought that I
dared to take his iconic road not taken long ago,
and here in cottage country Georgian Bay I've
kept my promises in anguished reverence for all
of my unexpected blessings, and I sit in peace
with my weary soul listening to the sounds
of nature contentedly reading poetry.

Conundrum

I didn't hear
the first sentence
in my mind, as often
happens when my Oracle
speaks to me, and I sit
and wait for inspiration;
but nothing happens.
Is that fair? I ask myself.
But who am I to question
the mystery of creation?
Philosophers, mystics,
and scientists alike cannot
solve the riddle of life,
and I pour my thoughts
down as if they were
my own; but are
they mine, or my
Oracle's?

The Devil's Shadow

"I'd rather read a thousand spiritual musings
than poetry. It's torture," said Penny Lynn
(my musings threaten the Devil's shadow);
but the more I explained "it" to her, the more
she desisted— "What I don't like about poetry
is that it's up to the individual to figure it out.
Why can't they be more explicit?" But when I
gave "it" to them on a golden platter worthy
of a noble prince— *"Tell it unveiled, the naked
truth, the declaration's better than the secret!"*
said the Sufi mystic—they could not swallow
"it" and spit it out—a hard truth to ingest; so I
stopped threatening the Devil's shadow and
gave "it" to them slanted— *"Success in circuit
lies,"* said the mystic Emily Dickinson—in
the more palatable form of poetry.

Memories of Her Past Life

The first time was a miraculous surprise,
the second time befuddling, and the third time
bizarre; but who can argue with the Voice
when it tells you to go to the casino?

"Go to the casino," said the Voice the first time,
but Penny resisted because she was working;
but the Voice insisted and told her again to go
to the casino, and still Penny resisted because
she had her job to do. But the third time the Voice
told her to go to the casino Penny relented, and
she came out of the Georgian Downs Casino nine
hundred and fifteen dollars richer, *and we
thought this was miraculous.*

"Go to the casino," said the Voice a second time
nine months later as she was driving to work one
morning; but this time Penny did not argue with the
Voice and came home from Georgian Downs Casino
three thousand seven hundred and eighty-five dollars
richer, *and we thought this was befuddling.*

"Go to the casino," said the Voice a third time
while Penny was eating her lunch at the Bark Park
in Wasaga less than a month later, which came as a
shock to her; and this time she came home from the
casino three grand wiser because now she knew without

a doubt that she had inner guidance watching over her, and her haunting past-life fear of monetary insecurity finally loosened its grip on her.

A Stain Upon His Soul

Terry cursed the small patch
of brown soil on his luscious
green lawn where his grass
refused to grow after all of his
love and attention. For seven
years his front lawn was marred
by that solitary patch of brown
that he re-seeded and tended
to with stubborn pride every
summer for three years before
he lost his patience and cursed
it like Jesus cursed the fig tree;
and like an ugly port-wine stain
upon the beautiful face of his
luscious lawn he let it be until
he could stand it no longer, and
upon that brown patch of cursed
soil he relented seven fresh rolls
of vibrant green sod and waited
defiantly to see if his grass would
die or grow. But sad to say, the
next summer his brown patch
came back to haunt him like
a stain upon his soul.

The Forbidden Teaching

Rumi's father Bahauddin confessed,
in *The Drowned Book,* that he practiced
the forbidden teaching of blissful union
with God through pleasure and desire—
"When I deeply know my senses, I feel
in them the way to God and the purpose
of living"—as did I in medieval Persia,
my past-life incarnation as Salaam the
Sufi who was pulled apart by the two
stallions of my life—my love for God
and sex; and in the twenty-third year of
my confused and lonely life I awakened
the *kundalini* by chance one night as I
meditated on a maple leaf in the Alpine
city of Annecy, and the *serpent fire* nearly
drove me mad again like it did in ancient
Persia, until I mastered the sacred art
of dying before dying.

The Poet and His English Teacher

"My story is not for the faint of heart,"
    wrote the ageing poet to his English teacher
fifty years after handing in his strange poem
    "Noman" that exploded from his unconscious
like a volcanic eruption, the molten words
    singeing the untried soul of his tender-green
educator; but the archetypal pattern of the poem
    had burned itself into the impressionable mind
of the newborn poet, and by chance someone
    answered his request on Social Media for his
old English teacher's address, and surprised that
    he was still alive sent him a copy of his memoir
that fulfilled his prophetic poem's imperative
    to find his lost soul; but his old high school
English teacher, who had to be in his nineties,
    did not respond to the poet's letter because
his story was even more shocking than his *daemonic*
    poem, "Noman" who had been summoned
to God for a reckoning of his cursed soul.

Time Traveler

*"There is no other place
to find yourself. Now is your only context,"*
said the bearded man in the miracle portrait
with the lamb in his arm and a lion cloud
in the pale blue sky—reincarnation doesn't matter,
nor does the hollow science that when the body
dies the self is no more; the only resolution
is the moment, forever the fertile womb
of the infinite universe.

He came from the future, the bearded man
in the miracle portrait, to open the strait gate to
a timeline of resolution; and for centuries the narrow
way of the living waters of destined purpose was
heeded; but the worm in the apple spoiled the
barrel, and the man from the future had
to come back again.

*"There is no other place
to find yourself. Now is your only context,"* he
repeated, and expounded upon the sacred mystery
of self-redemption, and the timeline of resolution
was re-affirmed upon the divine premise of accountable
effort; and when his portrait was completed, the bearded
man with the lamb in his arm returned to the future
and waits for the world to catch up to him.

Every Poet Is a Joyce

Every poet is a Joyce,
digging for the treasure in the field
with their spade of words;
and whether they find the treasure
depends upon the field
they're digging in.

Doors

Every door we open leads
to another world, but we don't
have enough life in us to open
every door; and if we did, what
good would it do us?

Unless we know the answer
to this question, every door remains
a mystery; but we open every door
to satisfy the longing in our soul.

I opened a door long ago
that led to a world of possibilities,
and I could have become affluent;
but it did not satisfy the longing
in my soul, and another door
opened up to me.

The world behind this door
was strangely familiar and exotic,
and I explored every corner to satisfy
the longing in my soul; and when I
left this strange world, I closed
the door behind me.

Homo Nuovo

Does it really matter that we can travel in time
if we have not become what we're meant to be? Time travel
only delays our destined purpose, and we must
always return to face the music.

And does it matter that we can teleport from here to there
when we're still the same person? We may have conquered
time travel and teleportation, a very secret agenda, but
does this help us fulfill our destined purpose?

Souls from other worlds have heeded the call to raise the
vibrations of life on earth to save our troubled planet, but
what does this tell us about who we are? Aren't
we free to change our karmic timeline?

It doesn't matter how much we evolve in mind and body,
the buck always stops with us, and not until we pay the piper
will *homo sapiens* stop evading his essential nature
and evolve into *homo nuovo*.

The Writer's Heart

His self-confident voice was redolent
with the wisdom of overcoming,
and every word he uttered
came from his soul, —

O victory!

Like a compulsive worm writhing
through the grime of urban life,
he slithered his lonely way
to new understanding, —

O victory!

One story led to another, easily
finding their way into the *New Yorker*,
and he elated with giddy delight
at his creations; but his story
never ended, —

O victory!

Always hovering near a greatness he
was too shrewd or diffident to risk,
he garnered the Pulitzer with ease;
but the Nobel always eluded his
gifted, covetous reach.

O misery!

When asked why on his deathbed, he
smiled bewilderment; but the twinkle
in his little rabbit's eye betrayed the
writer's heart, robbing Death of
its assured victory.

A Window

Sitting at my desk writing poetry
a window opened up to me, and
I saw what I could not have
seen many years ago.

The window opened onto a world
that looked the same as mine,
but only millions of years ahead
of our troubled time.

I saw reptilian beings far advanced
in mental powers and technology,
but they were less than human
in spiritual discernment.

And I saw another peculiar race
of ant-like creatures more evolved
than the reptilians, but they too
were spiritually insufficient.

I could not pull my eyes away;
but when I had seen enough of these
higher races, the window closed
and I returned to my poetry.

The Poet's Daemon

Is it cryptic or deceptive
when the poet conceals
what his *daemon* chooses
to reveal?

The poet does not know
what his poems will discover;
he goes in blind into the
caverns of his mind.

He may not find what he's
looking for, but he trusts
his *daemon* to light the way
to his hidden treasure.

That's the nature of the poet's
way, and he has no say in how
his *daemon* chooses to reveal
the wisdom of his poetry.

Envy

We love most
what we cannot have,
and envy those
that have it.

It is to our nature
to be this way,
but it doesn't have to be
if we are free.

This is our dilemma,
and not until we resolve
this inherency can we
love without envy.

Cycles of Life

Every life is a path
to the end of one's
beginning,

And every beginning
is a path to a new
way of living.

Redemption

Harnessed by vanity
she lost her spontaneity,
the greatest tragedy
of her life.

Where in God's name
did it come from,
this demon beast of
self-love?

Year after year
she sought an answer,
and then one day a voice
within spoke to her—

"Why do you lie?

She lied for self-love,
that was her only answer;
so she stopped lying and
got her life back again.

Meaning

Only meaning
will set us free
from the absurdity
of our existence.

But meaning
cannot be found
in the non-reality
of our being.

That's the irony of
being and non-being,
the soul of man's
dual nature,

and making the false
into the real makes us
whole and gives meaning
to our existence.

Cancer of the Soul

A negative attitude
 is like second-hand smoke,
causing cancer of the soul;
 but misery loves company,
and sour people refuse to
 sweeten. This was my new
friend's story, gratuitously
 fouling the air with cruel
insensitivities. But one day he
 crossed the line, calling his
wife a big fat stupid cow in front
 of me, and I had no choice
but to call him up on his rude
 behavior. This put our new
friendship into jeopardy, and
 sad to say my new friend in
Georgian Bay was too proud
 to change his negative ways,
and we parted company.

My Legacy

Memories
are the stuff of life,
the nurture of our soul,
and the better the memories
that we have, the happier we
will be when we get old;
and that's the only piece
of wisdom that I have
worth passing on.

Lunch at Moxie's

I had lunch at *Moxie's* in Barrie
    the other day with a very special
lady whose character fit the
    restaurant's name (which divine
serendipity had chosen for us) to
    a tee; fifty-two years old now and
mother of two respectful, loving
    children, still struggling with MS
(fifteen years now) but more than
    satisfied in her accomplishments:
a dream home on the lovely Niagara
    Escarpment, still married to the same
man who won her discerning heart,
    and a career that she loves more now
than when she started upon graduating
    with a B.Sc., from the University of
Windsor that I drove a thousand miles
    to bring her to every year, but no
longer needing confirmation for her own
    identity that her career and motherhood
have given her; she's free to live life on her
    terms now, and what a joy it was to see
how she has grown into the woman
    that I saw in my sister's spunky little
girl so many years ago.

Mending the Circle

You cannot mend a crack
in the basement by putting
new shingles on the roof,
nor can you fix a leaky faucet
by painting the living room,
or fix a broken relationship
by making new friends;
the circle has to be mended
where it has been broken,
or the soul will never
be whole.

Sensory Pleasure

Is this how I want to spend
my day, scratching an itch
that won't go away? —

I scratch and scratch my itch,
and it goes away, but it always
comes back again.

I could live my life
scratching—food, drink, sex,
whatever; but if I do, I'll go
to my grave unsatisfied, —

for such is the nature of
sensory pleasure!

Pinning the Devil Down

I hate it when a poet
tries to be profound with
what he does not know, forever
struggling to free himself from
his shallow grave;

and I hate it when a poet
tries to be cavalier with deadly
serious matters, making out
like he's above the fray;

and I hate it when a poet
assumes an air he has not earned,
wearing the poet's mantle
for authority;

and I hate it most when a poet
gets it right, because he's pinned
the Devil down and wrestled
all the wit, charm, and
deceit out of him!

Dogs of Desire

Every murder mystery writer
writes their story from back
to front, omniscient of all the
facts of their story, but we don't
know that; that's what makes
them a murder mystery story, —

And so is life a mystery story
like the murder mystery writer's
story, fraught with red herrings and
dead-ends, but who is the author
of this fabulous story? And how
do we solve this mystery without
an author to guide us? —

What if we work backwards, like
the author of the murder mystery
story? Can we follow the clues
from back to front and see the
big picture? But how can we
follow the clues from back to
front if we are dead? —

The case lingered...

As chance would have it, he found
a clue in something a poet said about
a man who went on a journey into

a desert and died of thirst but came
back to life again; and he studied
the mystical poet and his case
was resurrected, —

"Die before dying," wrote the mystic
poet, dropping his best clue, and he
embarked upon a journey into the
arid desert of his lost soul, and every
day another dog of desire died a sweet,
excruciating death—*how he craved
a single drop of water!* —

And the clues kept coming...

Emaciated, he kept searching for the oasis
of precious water, but it was so far away;
and when he lay down to rest his last dog
of desire sprang to life, and he dragged his
weary soul to the life-giving water and
died of sheer exhaustion—the final
clue that solved the mystery, —

Case closed!

Master Assembler

How easily we're intimidated
      by the man of knowledge, so much
information to grasp and understand,
      like British journalist/historian/artist
Paul Johnson, author of sixty books, not
      to mention his memoir (how many
volumes, we don't know) that he's working
      on; we wonder, where does it all
come from, all of this knowledge? And as I
      read his book *To Hell with Picasso
and Other Essays*, selected weekly columns
      that he wrote for the *Spectator*
(upon reading his book *Intellectuals* with
      fascination, especially "The Deep
Waters of Ernest Hemingway"), I saw that I
      had no need to be intimidated by his
vastly superior knowledge, because he's just
      a master assembler of historical facts
and information, and I just love reading
      how he puts it all together.

The Housefly

Washing out the coffee pot this
      morning, I woke up a big black
housefly and it buzzed frantically
      at the kitchen window looking
for a way out. I put the coffee pot
      down and picked up my dishcloth
and frantically tried to capture it;
      but the big black noisy housefly
was too fast for me. Yet I persisted,
      and almost caught it. Then it flew
under the window blinds and I could
      not get to it; but so frantic was the
fly that it buzzed into a lower corner
      of the window and I trapped it under
my damp dishcloth— "Gotcha!" For a
      fleeting moment my heart went out
to the poor creature, and I thought of
      taking it outdoors and setting it free;
but that was much too inconvenient,
      and I flushed it down the sink. Now
I'm so full of guilt for going against
      my better nature that I don't know
how to make up for it; and I can't help
      but feel that it was providentially
designed for that big black housefly
      that's floating around in our stinky
septic tank to be at our kitchen window
      this morning just to remind me how
highly evolved I am.

Somerset Maugham

False modesty or not,
I cannot say, but it certainly
was not true for me, the
confession he made at the age
of ninety that his life was of
no consequence, and that it
would have made no difference
to the universe had he never
existed, because a novel that he
wrote combusted a fire in my
soul that changed my life
forever; and to this day, half
a century later, I still marvel
at the effect *The Razor's Edge*
had upon me.

No More!

A day without focus is wasted,
a sin against telos; groggy,
stumbling, despair—

God, I miss running!

Not one, but two attacks
upon my tired heart, and then
a triple bypass—

God, I miss running!

My new normal haunts me,
vampire spirit without a ghost
sucking my life away—

God, I miss running!

The most rotten day,
I salvaged with a good run,
but no more, —

No more!

Distress

I went for a walk
down to the boardwalk
and sat on the viewing pod
overlooking Georgian Bay.

I did not ponder or reflect,
I just sat and watched
and listened to the gentle
waves rolling in.

Little whitecaps popped
up close to shore, over there
and there, and a gentle breeze
cooled my face.

I went for a walk
down to the boardwalk
to ease the burden
on my mind;

I watched the waves
rolling in, whitecaps smiling,
and my mind was eased
of my distress, —

I should walk more often.

Mixed Feelings

I saw a damaged soul
last night, a single woman
desperate to be loved
but couldn't love herself.

I saw a damaged soul
last night, a lonely young
man tearing his heart apart
denying his biology.

I saw a damaged soul
last night, a married man
going deaf to all the many
sounds of love.

Everywhere I looked
I saw another damaged soul,
and I went to bed not knowing
whether to laugh or cry.

Lifeblood

When I want inspiration
I turn to literature,
the lifeblood of human
experience.

Not music, nature, religion,
or—God forbid! another
elusive muse; just the lifeblood
of human experience.

Varied, mundane or complex,
poem, prose, essay, each written
in the lifeblood of human
experience.

Experience is the teacher,
guide, and lesson all rolled up
into one, the numinous spirit
of implacable wisdom, —

My inspiration!

There Is One Sin

There is one sin
that no one can speak of,
or even dare to think; a sin
so vile that even nature
shudders.

So deeply engrained is
this sin that no one can trace
where it came from, neither
scientist nor theologian.

Like a ghost, either male
or female, this sin imprisons
the soul and makes its new
body home;

And the body sins and sins
and sins without ceasing;
but all the guilt of sinning
kills soul's love of self,
and God, —

And the rest is commentary.

The Smell of Life

"I love the smell of this book,"
said Penny Lynn this morning.
"It smells of life."

She was reading the book
I stole from high school half
a century ago, *Great Short
Stories from the World's
Literature,* and had only forty
more pages to go.

But I wondered to myself
as I worked on my new book
Death, the Final Frontier,
was it the old musky library
book that smelled of life,
or the stories? —

The Snows of Kilimanjaro
stunk to high heaven of
Hemingway's self-betrayal,
The Wall by Sartre puissant
with the absurdity of life,
and *The Three Hermits* by
Tolstoy redolent with
lingering hope!

Efficiency

A lifetime of learning
has brought me to one simple
perspective, a life lesson
on efficiency, —

O saving grace!

It wasn't anything that I
had said or done, but what I
failed to finish, always
leaving bits of me to
reassemble, —

O misery!

A Writer's Lament

He wrote to shine like the sun
and be read throughout time,
sacrificing everyone for
his glorious dream, —

A desire he was born with,
a vision, ambition, pathology
that drove him to barter his
soul for recognition, —

But not without honor,
such was the integrity of his art
that he labored on relentlessly
with assiduous ardor, —

And he flew into the sun's
orbit, shining brightly for all
the world to see, but his wick
burned down too quickly, —

He wrote a memoir, grinding
one more axe; but his one true
love rose up to haunt him, and
he cried like a lost soul, —

He measured his great success
with his one true love, and
relenting his betrayal blew his
brains out with his shotgun.

The Letter

The clock started ticking
when she told me the news,
and my mind went numb
with horrifying fear.

Nothing mattered anymore,
not even breakfast, lunch
or dinner, all the universe
shouted the end was near.

The clock is still ticking,
and my dreams came to a
braking halt, regardless of
a good or bad result.

Harvard Boy

Achievement standing in for meaning,
fast-tracking to a life not meant to be
for Harvard Boy, —

Lawyer, father, uncle, aunt, cousin,
family meme, when life interrupted HB's
achievement and deflected his journey
to mystic self-discovery, —

OOPS!

Loss of vision in one eye playing the sacred
game, and Thoreau came calling, —

Sixteen months of snail-paced silence, no
phone, radio, or TV, and fearing loss of
mind and self HB returned to Boston—
family, friends, community! — replete
with Thoreau-like wisdom, and he
played the game of life with
one good eye open.

Stairway of Heaven

Poetry is the way
to the great reconciliation,
slashing through the forests
of our brambled self.

Every word, image, and experience
shines a light into the darkness
of tomorrow, leaving a trail
for us to follow.

No one poet knows the way
to the end of our becoming, but
every poem that he writes adds
a new rung to the stairway
of heaven, — the great
reconciliation!

Making Music

What's life for if not living?
and what's living if not doing?
and what's doing if not engaging
in what life calls us to do?

Ten-year-old Luca was called
to drumming, and pleading with
his parents was given a set
of drums for Christmas.

Luca plays his drums every day
after school now and whenever the
spirit moves him, because more
than anything else he loves
making music, —

And that's what life is for!

Philosopher's Stone

The object, the image that never
went away, always grabbing attention
to validate identity, as though the object
did not exist if not noticed, —

Why?

The object exists no less than a rock,
mountain, or stream; why must I always
stand where everyone must see me? —

Surely!

Suffering, loss, humiliation saved the day,
no more attention, flattery, or rejection;
only the essence of my image, —

A marriage of ego and humility!

New Age Religion

Like a carrot on a stick, a New Age Religion
    with its ever-ready Master (both Inner
and Outer) promises safe haven from every
    decision, a potpourri of purloined wisdom
exotically articulated to sound like a fresh
    mountain stream mercifully pouring out
of the mouth of God, Light and Sound divine,
    sacred HU so full of promise only a fool
would refuse to call upon the sacred name;
    but as hard as every chela tries to satisfy
the longing in their soul, forever striving for
    the next initiation (a Fifth Initiate becomes
a member of the secret Order of the Oak), the
    carrot on the stick is always always always
beyond the reach of the inveigled believer
    and robs them of the freedom to bear
the exquisite fruit of their own tree.

Karma

It's ironic, the way we grow
    into who we are, putting on
more and more identity with
    what we do, day in and day
out, pound after pound of ego,
    never noticing how fat we
get until we can no longer bear
    the weight of who we are
and suffer all the pains that come
    with age; and then we shed
those pounds away as the light
    of day begins to fade, and
if we're lucky we will die as
    innocent as when we came,
but only much wiser.

Specter of the Project

Have you ever wondered why it's so hard to start a project your heart is not into but you have to do it because if you don't it will cost you to have it done professionally, not that a pro would do a better job than you who has done it before two or three times, but the cost isn't necessary, not yet anyway, and it hurts to pay a professional for what you can do yourself, but you can't get started because all of that psychic energy of the finished project stands like a specter of congealed stasis at the beginning of your project, and you just can't get the damn thing started no matter how hard you try!

Jehovah's Witnesses at My Door

Dick and Mary ("Not Dick and Jane," he said)
came to my door this morning (I was sitting
on the deck reading WRITING IN GENERAL AND
THE SHORT STORY IN PARTICULAR,), Jehovah's
Witnesses, a lovely couple about to celebrate
their 60th wedding anniversary, a long time to
be together, and Mary had the loveliest smile
(which I made a point of telling her) and Dick
as content as could be in their missionary zeal,
and I listened, not out of courtesy but out of
respect for their age and commitment, and we
talked for twenty minutes about the end of times
and free will (I championed free will, they the
Bible) and world events and other things, but
mostly sticking to their closed script, and when
they left smiling at their surprising reception I
read their two WATCHTOWER pamphlets ("Has
Science Replaced the Bible" and "Your Cells Living
Libraries!") and opened the book that Dick wanted
me to read, WHAT DOES THE BIBLE REALLY TEACH?
and started reading, not that I was thinking of
converting, but because I told Dick and Mary I
would read it, but nineteen pages into the glossy
little book and I had to put it aside because it
was too hard to swallow; nice people Dick
and Mary, but an absurd religion.

The Messenger

There's a calm tenacity to his words,
A power beyond endurance, but
so light are his thoughts to him that
he doesn't even notice.

When he speaks, he seems the same
as you and me; but at some point in
the conversation his demeanor changes,
and he's off to higher places.

Words flow from his mouth like fresh
spring water, and what was light,
easy, and ordinary now becomes
mystical with sacred meaning.

"It's like God sent you," they all say,
when he finishes speaking; and he smiles
and says, "I know. But that's what
you needed to hear, —"

And everything returns to normal.

Ode to the Poet

"God," said I, "be my help and stay secure;
I'll think of the Leech Gatherer on the
lonely moor!" wrote Wordsworth,
lighting my soul on fire, —

Every poet explores their own stage
on this journey through life, not yours
or mine, but their own rendition of
the messy human condition, —

But not unlike yours or mine, the poet
speaks to every soul, and we look to
poetry to confirm our own place
in the cosmic journey, —

Some poets are obscure, some recondite;
but esoteric or mesoteric, every poem
administers one more truth to heal
our soul and set us free from the
ennui of our lonely journey.

By Their Voice We Know Them

There are two women that I know,
not personally but on the CBC,
both very charming in their smiling
voice but hollow in their tone.
They have no idea they're so phony
and behave like normal people,
but I can hear the falseness in their
smiling voice, and it drives me crazy.
I try and try to like these women,
their shows being so appealing,
but the infidelity in their smiling
voice can wear their show thin. For
years I've listened to these women,
one weekend mornings, the other
Sundays at two, but time alone
cannot make them true and now
they just amuse me.

Child Brody

The veil parted, and three-year-old
Child Brody entered the magical kingdom
far away from all the confusion of the
world where his grandparents lived and
the five senses ruled the body and starved
the famished soul, —

Hungry for affection, Child Brody ran
across the street and found new friends and
played and laughed and played and laughed,
telling his grandmother to go home when
she came to get him for dinner, —

"Go home, go home" the child insisted, and
his grandfather too when he crossed the street
with a goblet of wine and bigger scowl. "Go home," he
said, pushing at his grandfather's knee, because
they did not belong in his magical kingdom
where he was free to be Child Brody.

Smoothies

To have a desire without the need
is a very strange feeling, but that's
what smoothies do to me, —

I make one every morning, kale,
orange, banana, other fruits and seeds
to satisfy my nutritional needs, —

And the rest of the day I suffer from
empty desire, a hollow feeling of
wanting without need, —

A healthy place to be!

Biography of a Lesbian Poet

There's a bit of the weasel in her
that only the Single Eye can see,
trying to deceive the Gatekeeper
of the Kingdom with clever poetry;
but to enter into the mystic circle
of Singularity, only truth untarnished
by ego personality will do, the only
coin in the Eternal Realm with
true currency.

The Making of an Atheist

She stared out her living room window
lost to the world she knew and loved, three
hours later she returned from the farthest
regions of her mind where the great void
swallowed her whole, and she gave the rest
of her life to helping others, founding a home
for unwed mothers and an AIDS hospice for
gays among many other charitable causes,
and all because a drunken driver had run
over her golden boy. She went to church and
knelt for hours begging God to tell her why
her twenty-year old son had to die, but God
did not respond and she walked away with
her unyielding pride leaving her simple faith
that she had inherited from her caring mother
and philandering father who had abandoned
her when she was twelve behind her. "Saint
Joan," they called her, for all her good works,
and they named a street after her when
she died of inoperable cancer.

Duende

The young child at play,
that's *duende*;

The magic of Harry Potter,
that's *duende*;

Dancing in the rain,
that's *duende*;

Songs that make you cry,
that's *duende*;

The Mona Lisa smile,
that's *duende*;

Holding your lover's hand,
that's *duende*;

Crossing the finishing line,
that's *duende*;

And an old farmer dying in grace,
that's *duende*, the sacred
mystery of everything.

Bad News

Is there ever a good time
for bad news, like the day
before my birthday and long
July weekend, summer perfect,
weather we've waited all year
for? But bad news really has no
season, coming when the gods
decree, and there's nothing we
can do but deal with it; but not
right away. One needs time to
heal from the blow before one
rallies the wounded soul.

The Stuff of Life

Betrachten is a German word, and
very difficult to translate, but it means
impregnating with attention, like the
book Penny Lynn is reading that bores her
to distraction because it lacks *betrachten*,
that special quality that she intuitively
identified as the stuff of life, —

The mystery of *betrachten* is about conception,
speaking to the élan vital of every living thing,
and it is transmitted by infusing with attention
not unlike making love but only spiritually,
giving living élan like the joy every child
experiences when playing with its mother
whose attention is pure bliss, —

"This book lacks story," said Penny Lynn, unable
to fathom the mystery of its boring nature, but
the story her book lacked was the élan of its
divine nature, the vital soul of the author's telos,
academic, dry, and desolate of pure intention,
the Divine Creator in all of us whose attention
gives life to you, me, books, and everything, the
I Am that I Am principle that the German people,
who also gave us the shame of the Holocaust,
call *betrachten* and Penny Lynn calls the stuff
of life, the eternal story of our becoming,
and the mystery of our being.

My Quandary for the Day

I don't know if the end is near,
though life makes me want to feel
this way some days, and there are
other days when life makes me
want to feel like I can never die;
but I know better than to play into
these feelings and go with what
my body tells me instead, which is
more than what I care to think
about because I neither want to
leave this world nor stay, and that's
my quandary for the day.

Peach Cobbler

He walked over with his drink of rye,
returning the tea towel she had used to
carry over her oven-warm peach cobbler
the other day, and sat down with me in
the shade of the maple tree where I was
reading the Freud/Jung letters to satisfy
my curiosity on the private relationship
of the founding fathers of psychotherapy,
my preference by far for Jung who became
my hero of the *secret way* that he brought
into the open with his gnostic *psychology
of individuation,* and taking a gulp of rye,
idiosyncratic to annoyance, preferential
eater and scoffer of all foods foreign to
his palate (how would he know if he does
not try them?), proceeded to offer his
opinion on Jung's painful break with his
mentor, uninformed and fatuous, and
I inquired about the cobbler, expecting
him to be polite whether he liked it or
not; but he chose not to lie and told me
it was too sweet for his liking, egregious
cognitive dissonance for a man whose
whole life was a lie, but that's how the
shadow plays, always dancing to the tune
of self-serving logic in the hope of finding
a partner to dance with. "Oh well," said I,
smiling at his little game; "it was a new
recipe, and you were our neighborly
guinea pigs."

A Sacred Contract

Life is all about negotiating our way
from here to there, wherever
there may be, for reasons
we think we know but are never
quite certain, —

Life is all about compromise,
small, big, and bigger, and if we
cross the line to the nether side
of the great divide, we forfeit
our right to be, —

Life is all about redemption,
reclaiming the I we compromised
to the I we are not, and life goes
on from life to life, a sacred contract
to the end of time.

Tribute to Emily

In art as in life
the word sounds loud
when context can be found;
ferreting the meaning of context,
the word sounds out.

Out stepped the other
from the same old desire,
only to stomp on innocence
with devilish glee, —

O destiny, o destiny!

The wine tastes bitter, and the
meat sour, but the body hungers
for more; sounding out the word,
a new creature is born, —

O Emily!

The Circus Never Stops

In the dusty, bloodied, and tear-soaked
arena of daily confrontations with life
and not the catacombs of the Bibles,
Korans, and Gospels of the world
will we find ourselves, —

Lost in a haze of wonder, not knowing
which path to take, life comes crashing down,
and a new way is found to the promised
land of undreamt horizons, and new
joys and miseries ensue, —

The circus never stops, day in and day out
the monkeys play, and Old Whore Life
laughs, and laughs, and laughs until
the hammer comes crashing
down again, —

And a new way is found!

INTERVIEW WITH THE AUTHOR

Sunday, February 5, 2017
Georgian Bay, Ontario

PP: *If I may begin, what are your impressions of poetry?*
OS: Poetry puzzles everyone, including the poets. I myself, who found the sacred knowledge of the secret way—the path to one's true self—am intrigued by the gnostic wisdom that characterizes poetry; but not until one has seen the blueprint of our destined purpose will one solve the mystery that is the undiscovered soul of poetry. Having said this, you may ask me whatever you wish to know about me.

PP: *What do you mean by the blueprint of our destined purpose?*
OS: Every soul is encoded with God's DNA. That's the blueprint of our destined purpose, and the telos of our existence. It may be hard to believe, but there it is.

PP: *Are you saying that we are all a part of God?*
OS: That's exactly what I'm saying.

PP: *And by telos you mean that we are destined to become God-like?*
OS: The poet William Wordsworth said that we all come from God, trailing clouds of glory; and John Keats intuited that our purpose in life is to realize our own identity, "a bliss peculiar to each by individual existence." And Emily Dickinson wrote: "Adventure most unto itself /The Soul condemned to be; /Attended by a Single Hound— /Its own Identity." Why is it so hard for people to see that we are all sparks of God born to

realize our own divine nature, our true identity as the poets intuited? Are we afraid to know ourselves?

PP: *Fascinating. And how would one realize their divine nature?*

OS: That's the mystery; isn't it? That's what keeps poets writing. The way to one's true self is the undiscovered soul of poetry, and all art. All of life for that matter, because the way to one's true self is everywhere to be found. That's why people turn to poetry when they feel lost. Poetry shines a light on one's path, because the poet is the light-giver on the way to one's true self. That's the poet's purpose, whether they know it or not. Why do you think poets *have* to write their poems? Writers are always talking about truth-finding; but what is this truth they are seeking if not the way to one's true self? That's the genius of poetry. It shines a light upon every person's path, whatever one's path may be; because the way to one's true self is the same for you as it is for me. Carl Jung said in *The Red Book* that this life is the way to the unfathomable which we call divine, all other ways are false paths. What did he mean by this? Your life, my life, his or her life—we are all our own way to our true self. That's the mystery that runs through *Not My Circus, Not My Monkeys*. I know the secret way, but I can't tell anyone openly. I'd be scorned for my presumption. Why do you think Emily Dickinson wrote, "Tell the truth, but tell it slant, /Success in circuit lies"?

PP: *Yes. "The truth must dazzle gradually /Or every man be blind." But why? Why do poets have to be so mystical? Why couch the truth of life in metaphor and symbol? Why can't poetry be straight-talking?*

OS: Do you think poets do this intentionally? Of course they don't. They are servants of their muse, and what their muse gives them they must write. The real question should be: *what is this mysterious muse that inspires poetry?* When I'm called to write a poem, I don't know what my poem is going to say. A line may come to me out of the blue, or maybe two or three lines, and then I have to work out the rest of the poem. The poem seems to exist somewhere already in the great unconscious, and it's my job to get it out the way it wants to be expressed. That's the work part of writing poetry. It's a two-way street. We're seldom given the entire poem. That only happened to me once when I was in high school. I woke up one morning in the grips of my *daemon*, and I wrote an entire poem called *Noman* that not only blew my English teacher's mind but puzzled me most of my life. It took fifty years before I made sense of that poem, and I wrote a book to explain it. *The Summoning of Noman*. But that's a long story, and if anyone's interested they can read the book. So there's more to writing poetry than meets the eye.

PP: *So you started writing poetry in high school?*

OS: Yes. But I wanted to be a prose writer like my high school hero Ernest Hemingway. Then in grade twelve I read Somerset Maugham's novel *The Razor's Edge,* and I was called to a different path.

PP: *What path would that be?*

OS: Maugham's hero Larry Darrell became a truth seeker because he wanted to know the meaning and purpose of life. I was called to the same path and became a truth seeker too. Ironically, that's the same path that writers are called to; but my calling was more specific. I had to find my own entry into the undiscovered country of my soul, and I found Gurdjieff's teaching. That's the path that initiated me into the mysteries of the secret way. You see, the secret way is there for everyone to find; but the secret way will only reveal itself to one who dares to live their own life, the life they are called to live that Robert Frost pointed to in his poem "The Road Not Taken." This is the sacred mystery of the secret way that took me years to penetrate. Only by being true to yourself can the sacred knowledge reveal itself to you. Once again, this is the mystery of poetry. This is why the incomparable literary critic Professor Harold Bloom was enraptured by poetry so early in life and never stopped loving it. Poetry spoke to his soul and haunted him his whole life, especially Hart Crane's poetry, but he could never satisfy the longing in his soul that poetry points to.

PP: *Have you satisfied the longing in your soul?*

OS: Yes.

PP: *Can you define this longing? And is it the same for every soul?*

OS: It's the same longing for every soul, and it's the longing to be our true self; but we cannot become our true self until we forfeit our false self. But now we're getting into some really deep waters, and I'm not so sure I want to go there.

PP: *You did give me carte blanche?*

OS: Fair enough. Ask away, then.

PP: *Let's talk about you. What makes you tick?*

OS: Wow! What makes me tick? I've never given that any thought, really. I've always taken myself for granted, and by that I mean that I knew I was born for a purpose, and it was up to me to figure out what this purpose was.

PP: *And did you figure it out?*

OS: As absurdly simple as it may be, yes: I was born to become myself. This of course presupposes my whole life's quest, because I spent the best and most creative years of my life looking for the real me. Let me see if I can put this in a way that won't sound so abstruse. A very strange thing happened to me in high school. I think it happened either in the latter part of grade nine, or sometime in grade ten, something that changed my life in a way that I never understood but which was probably why Maugham's novel *The Razor's Edge* spoke to me in grade twelve. I had a subtle shift in my personality, a shift in my psyche that gave me a feeling of being false, of not being genuine, true, and authentic. I would get these impulses to be false every now and then, especially when I was put on the spot by someone, and this feeling haunted me from the first time I became conscious of my falseness. But then this feeling gradually took over my whole personality, and I no longer realized that I was being false except in exceptional circumstances when I felt strongly compelled to lie or cheat or pretend to be what I was not; and that's when guilt possessed me and I hated myself. So I became a truth seeker because I wanted to find the real me that I had lost in high school. The real me was pervaded by this inexplicable feeling of falseness, and I had no idea where it came from until I discovered reincarnation and studied Edgar Cayce. I worked this out in my book *The Summoning of Noman*. Every time we're born into a new life, we create a new and separate personality; and with each new personality that we create we also create a false shadow side with all the unresolved karma that we repress to our unconscious. But when we die, our personality does not die with our body; we bring all of our personalities with us into our next incarnation, but we're not conscious of them. As we grow in our new incarnation, we create a new and distinct personality out of our new genetic make-up and environment; but our old personalities seep into our new personality. Well, sometimes our old personalities can seep so much into our new personality that they can have a great influence upon us. That's what I think happened to me in high school. I think—no, I don't think it; I *know* this is what happened to me. The repressed shadow self of all my past-life personalities—and by shadow self, I mean the unresolved karmic ego-energy of all my past lives, which constitutes the *non-being* of our ontological nature; well, this unresolved false self seeped into my evolving personality until it pervaded my psyche so thoroughly that it became my center of gravity. In effect, I became so false that I did not realize my own inauthenticity until many years later when I began to "work" on myself with Gurdjieff's teaching, and it was this ontological matrix of my own *non-being* (primarily driven by the debauched personality of my past lifetime in 17th Century Paris, France) that compelled me one night to have a sexual experience that shocked my conscience awake and catapulted me into my quest for my true self which formally began in Annecy, France where I went to live for a year. Wow! I thought I was going to give you a simple answer, but look where my *daemon* has taken me?

    PP: *What do you mean by daemon?*

OS: My *daemon* is my creative spirit, the unconscious creative side of my soul. I never know where it's going to take me, but I trust it implicitly.

PP: *Since you've opened this door, tell me more about this false self that man creates with every new incarnation. What do you mean by false self?*

OS: Oh gosh. I don't know if I want to go there."

PP: *It might help to explain your poetry. You do puzzle readers.*

OS: And with good reason.

PP: *Please explain.*

PP: I don't know if I can. I tried to open up the *way* for my reader with my four volumes of spiritual musings—my favorite is still my third volume, *Stupidity Is Not a Gift of God*; but that failed miserably. That's why I decided to write poetry instead. But given the response I got to my poems on my blog, I can see that I'm no further ahead. Perhaps I might have better luck with short stories. I'll have to wait and see. I've started to publish stories on my blog from my book *Sparkles in the Mist*. It's a collection of stories drawn from my life.

PP: *You haven't answered my question. What do you mean by false self?*

OS: Everyone has a false self. That's an ontological fact of life. We are both our *being* and *non-being*, whether we like it or not; but try proving that we *are* what we are not. That's the paradox of our nature that St. Paul called the *"selfsame thing."* Why do you think Shakespeare continues to haunt Professor Bloom? "To be, or not to be, that is the question" said Hamlet; and all of Shakespeare's plays are haunted by this question of our *being* and *non-being*. No one is exempt from the conflict of our paradoxical nature. We are all torn in two by the natural process of evolution, but nature cannot resolve the dilemma of our *"selfsame thing."* "Man must complete what nature cannot finish," said Carl Jung, quoting the ancient Gnostics; and he spent his life trying to resolve this dilemma. He did find a way out, but few people understand him. Only a poet would understand, he told his friend Miguel Serrano in Serrano's book *C. G. Jung and Hermann Hesse, A Record of Two Friendships*; so I'm not so sure I want to go there. What's the point if no one understands?

PP: *Well, you did say somewhere that you are writing for posterity.*

OS: Funny. Alright, let's go into the undiscovered country of my soul—or, I should say, the *discovered* country of my soul, because I did find my true self. That's the mystery here. That's what you want me to talk about, isn't it?

PP: *Yes.*

OS: Why? Why do you want me to open myself up to ridicule? Did you not read the epigraph to *Not My Circus, Not My Monkeys*? "Many pioneers can tell a story of misery, all due to the primitive misoneism of their contemporaries," said Carl Jung in his book *The Undiscovered Self*; so what makes you think that my outside-the-box perspective will have any more resonance than Jung's psychology of individuation which, incidentally, I think is still so far ahead of its time that it'll take society another fifty years to catch up to it. I don't need the misery.

PP: *Why did you write this book of poems, then?*

OS: It's my Ariadne's string out of Plato's cave.

PP: *Amusing. Okay, I get your point. But having found your true self, are you still compelled to write? As I understand your books, when one has resolved the paradox of their being and non-being one is no longer driven by the need to satisfy the longing in their soul which writers seek to do with their writing. You have satisfied the longing in your soul, so why do you continue writing? Why not leave well enough alone?*

OS: What the hell else am I going to do? I have a heart condition that prohibits physical activity, but I've still got a few more years to put in before I cross over, and I have to do something; so I write to keep myself busy, and sane I might add. It's a crazy world out there. That's why I titled my book *Not My*

Circus, Not my Monkeys. Do you see the irony? But I'm being obstreperous. I apologize. Let me answer your question, if I can. Let me answer it with my mixed metaphor of Ariadne's string and Plato's cave. Would that be okay?

PP: *I look forward to your answer.*

OS: You do realize that this goes to the very core of our existence?

PP: *I do, because I've read your books; but your reader may not know. So if you would, please explain it for posterity.*

OS: You make me laugh. Alright, let's do it for posterity. The first question you asked me was about the blueprint of our destined purpose. As I said, this goes to the core of our existence. I have no desire to prove this, because it can't be proven; it can only be experienced to be believed, so I won't waste my energy trying to prove that we are all sparks of God encoded with God's DNA for the divine purpose of realizing a new "I" of God. That's the blueprint of our destined purpose. We are all born for the purpose of creating a new "I" of God through the natural process of evolution through life; but, as Jung came to realize, the psyche is forever in the process of individuating the Self, and that's what we're born to do from one lifetime to the next until we break the chain of karma and reincarnation. There, I've said it; but who is going to believe that our purpose in life is to expand the consciousness of God by giving birth to God with every new "I" of God? Do you see my dilemma?

PP: *Yes, the God question. That always stops one in their tracks, doesn't it? It didn't stop you, though. Let's talk about the God question first, then. Your belief in God is unimpeachable. Can you tell me why?*

OS: I came into this world with a firm belief in God, but I was always puzzled why I believed in God when some of the best minds in the world didn't; like the existentialist philosopher Jean Paul Sartre, and Albert Camus whose writing I loved more than Sartre's, and big thinkers like Nietzsche and Lord Bertrand Russell whose book *Why I Am Not a Christian* led many people down the garden path. It took many years before I could find a solution to this problem—and man's belief or non-belief in God is a problem, because no one knows why some of us believe in God and others don't; but it finally came to me when I resolved the paradox of our *being* and *non-being*. I finally came to see that although man is forever in the process of *becoming* his true self through the natural process of karma and reincarnation, his belief or non-belief in God will always depend upon where his center of gravity is; and by center of gravity I mean our reflective self—our "I", if you will. If one's "I" is centered in his *being*, he will automatically believe in God because God is the ground of all BEING; but if one's "I" is centered in his *non-being*, one will automatically not believe in God, because the consciousness of our *non-being* is a consciousness of what we are not, and what we are not does not allow for a belief in our immortal soul, which is an immortal atom of God. I know this from personal experience because I had seven past-life regressions, and in one of my regressions I was brought back to the Body of God where all souls come from. But what made this regression pivotal in my understanding of the blueprint of our destined purpose was that as an atom of God I did not have reflective self-consciousness. I had to go through the natural process of evolution through life to give birth to my reflective self-consciousness, which I also experienced in that same regression when I was brought back to my first primordial human lifetime where I gave birth to my reflective self, a new "I" of God, if you will; but who in the world would believe this? Do you see my problem? I may get away with this in my writing, like my book *Death, the Final Frontier*; but this perspective is so far outside the box that people will scoff at it. But I don't mind, really; because like Gurdjieff used to say, "there is only self-initiation into the mysteries of life." Ironically, this was one mystery that Gurdjieff failed to experience, which is why he believed that man was not born with an immortal soul but could create one if he knew how. But I've dealt with this issue in my book *Gurdjieff Was Wrong, But His Teaching Works*, so I won't pursue it here. The question was, why do I believe in

God? Well, like Carl Jung replied to John Freeman in the now-famous *Face to Face* BBC interview when he was asked if he believed in God, "I don't need to believe; I know." Take it for what you will, but I'm one of the lucky birds in the Sufi Allegory *Conference of the Birds* that completed their spiritual quest and looked into the Face of God; I not only believe in God; I *know* that God Is. That's my reality.

PP: *Fair enough. And whether one believes you or not will depend upon where their I is centered in their ontological nature. But at least now we have it for posterity.*

OS: Yes. But let's explain this, shall we? I don't want to leave the impression that we are all centered in our *being* or *non-being*; that's not the way the natural process of individuation through karma and reincarnation works. We are forever in the process of *becoming* our true self, so we shift our center of gravity from our *being* to our *non-being* throughout the day. This is why we experience highs and lows in life, a dichotomy that launched Colin Wilson's literary career with his book *The Outsider* but which he was unable to resolve seventy books later. It can so happen however, that some of us get stuck in our *non-being* and don't realize it. This is what happens to people who are firmly fixed in their non-belief in God, people like Richard Dawkins and Christopher Hitchens. These people became so fixed in the consciousness of their *non-being* that God could not possible exist for them—

PP: *If I may interrupt you, what can one do about this? If one is so fixed in the consciousness of their non-being, how can one extricate oneself? This is where Gurdjieff's teaching came to your rescue, isn't it?*

OS: Yes. To answer your question, when one's center of gravity is so firmly fixed in their *non-being* they will suffer unbearable spiritual anguish; and not until one can bear it no longer will one look for a way out of their misery. I'd like to believe otherwise, but this was forced upon me by all the books I read, not only literature, but books on philosophy, psychology, and religion; and my own struggle to liberate myself, of course. Man has to bottom out of his own life before he looks for a way out of his misery. But this only makes sense in light of karma and reincarnation, which ironically one would not believe in if they are centered in their *non-being*. That's the tragedy of the inherent conflict in our soul, which I did my best to illustrate with my book *The Lion that Swallowed Hemingway*. Hemingway was so afflicted with his dark shadow self that he became impossible to suffer. Incidentally, I'm working on a sequel to my Hemingway book. It's called *My Writing Life*."

PP: *This is why you wrote that life can be cruel but ultimately fair, because man will always have a chance to redeem himself in another life. Hemingway couldn't do it, and he killed himself; but not your hero Dr. Jung who reclaimed his lost soul.*

OS: Exactly. Can we move on to something else? I fear we've gone way too far with this God issue. This isn't something one should talk about, because the question of God is very personal and we all come to our own answer accordingly.

PP: *Alright. Let's talk about your personal life. Your writing habits, your personal interests, and whatever else you want to say about yourself.*

OS: I don't mind talking about my personal life, but let me tell you why I wrote this book of poetry first. We digressed into the God question, so I never got to tell you that *Not My Circus, Not My Monkeys* is my Ariadne's string out of Plato's Cave. I wanted to give the reader a way out of their conflicted nature.

PP: *Are you saying that the poems in* Not My Circus, Not My Monkeys *are your Ariadne's string that will lead one out of Plato's cave? That's a tall order, don't you think?*

OS: Not if the reader takes what Emily Dickinson called "the clue divine."

PP: *St. Paul told us to work out our own salvation—with fear and trembling he added, to our dismay; is that what you mean by clue divine?*

OS: Yes, but with a little more help. As insightful as St. Paul may be on the secret teachings of the *way*, he's still too abstruse for most people, as is Emily Dickinson. That's why I wrote *Not My Circus, Not My Monkeys*. I poured the old wine into new bottles and brought the secret teachings of the *way* into the 21st Century.

PP: *You also make me laugh. Nonetheless, you have cast your bread upon the waters and there's no turning back now; so, can you be a little more explicit about your mixed metaphor of Ariadne's string and Plato's cave?*

OS: What can I say? Where do I start? This is what it's all about, isn't it? How long did it take you in your own path of suffering and glory to put off the *"old man"* and put on the *"new man"*, if I may allude to St. Paul's teaching?

PP: *This is not about me, it's about you. Your readers would like to know who you are and how you became who you are. Let's go back to the beginning, if you don't mind. You became interested in reading at an early age, did you not?*

OS: Yes, in grade school. I went to St. Edward's Roman Catholic School in my hometown of Nipigon, in Northwestern Ontario. I don't know which grade, but I would think grade seven for sure, because by the time I got to grade eight I tried to read one book every day, which I did for a long time. But now that I think of it, this was a very strange time in my life because I had the strangest feeling that there was a hole in my soul that I had to fill with reading; but I couldn't. I just couldn't, and no matter how much I read I still felt empty. It was an insatiable hunger that to this day has never really gone away. I still read voraciously, like I can never get enough knowledge; but curiously enough, I'm no longer driven by my hunger for knowledge, not since I discovered the sacred knowledge of the secret *way*. Once I discovered the sacred knowledge of the secret *way* I began to fill the hole in my soul, and I filled it to my complete satisfaction when I experienced my immortal self in my mother's kitchen one day while she was kneading bread dough on the kitchen table. But I've made reference to this already. I only want to say that from the earliest age I had a hunger for knowledge of a special kind, which I did not recognize until I ferreted out the secret *way* with Gurdjieff's teaching. Wow! Thank you for this. I had forgotten about how I tried to fill that hole in my soul with all the books I felt compelled to read. I still love to read, and I'm always putting new books on my Amazon wish list; but my reading is different now. I read to see how the *way* reveals itself, especially in poetry and literature because this is the best way for the *way* to illustrate the *enantiodromiac* process of the human condition.

PP: *Enantiodromiac process? That sounds ominous. What do you mean?*

OS: Well, I have a theory about reading now. I think people read the books they read because they are called to the *way* according to their spiritual need, and the books they read satisfy this need. And as they grow in their spiritual nature, in their own *becoming,* their immortal self that they create out of the *enantiodromiac* conflict of their *being* and *non-being* they will be attracted to different literature. For example, I was called by my spiritual need to read Maugham's novel *The Razor's Edge* in grade twelve, because this was the book I needed to begin my quest for my true self; and then in university serendipity introduced me to Ouspensky's book *In Search of the Miraculous,* which brought Gurdjieff's teaching into my life that opened me up to the secret way of life; so you see, the level of our spiritual need determines how much the secret way of life reveals itself to us. But this is so abstruse that I don't think anyone will understand what I'm trying to say. Why don't you tell me what you think?

PP: *As I said, this is not about me; but I know what you mean. Life is a journey of the self, and every self is different; so it would follow that we all have different needs. I agree; we read the books we read because this is how the way speaks to us. But this is difficult to explain. And yet, this is what* Not My Circus, Not My Monkeys *tries to do. Your poetry tries to give the reader an*

Ariadne's string to find their way out of Plato's cave of shadows and illusion. This is a hard message; but who knows who will be called to read your book? As you said, one does not choose the books they read; they choose the reader.

OS: Wonderful! Now we've really strayed into cloud-cuckoo-land! Don't you find it ironic, that when one gets too close to the truth it becomes too hard to swallow?

PP: *It's been forever thus. But isn't this the premise of Plato's allegory of the cave, that when one is brought too close to the light of the sun one's eyes are blinded?*

OS: "The truth must dazzle gradually /Or every man be blind," said Emily Dickinson. This is my entry into something that I wanted to say but couldn't, because the dialectic of this interview took us to cloud-cuckoo-land; but now I can say something about the truth of poetry and literature that needs to be said, something that I was called to from the earliest age but did not become conscious of until I found the secret way in everyday life. So, if you don't mind; I'd like to say something about *the living way*—

PP: *The living way? I've got goosebumps!*

OS: Don't make me laugh. As you very well know, I've read a lot of literature on teachings of the *way* as it has been expressed in various cultures; but not once in all the literature that I have read has anyone ever explained what the *way* really is. It's been called the Path, the Word, Logos, Spirit, Providence, Tao, Baraka, Chi, life force, and other names all expressing the various levels of cultural understanding. Hemingway even called it "the secret that is poetry written into prose," and Norman Mailer also sensed *the living way* in what he called "the spooky art of writing," but of all the writers that I have read only two ever penetrated the mystery—Emily Dickinson and the Sufi mystic Rumi. Shakespeare, Wordsworth, and Keats came dangerously close, and there are probably other poets who have, maybe Rilke from what I've read about him; but I can't be sure until I read him. Nonetheless, the point I want to make is that *the living way* is what compels writers to write and readers to read, because *the living way* is the way out of the paradox of one's *being* and *non-being*. I know this is really pushing the envelope, but *the living way* is God's love in action; it is how God brings soul back home to God through the natural process of soul's *becoming*—or, as Jesus expressed it in his teachings of the secret way, making our two selves into one. This is the underlying theme of my twin soul book, *The Merciful Law of Divine Synchronicity*.

PP: *The paradox of being and non-being, you mean?*

OS: Yes. The *"selfsame thing"* becoming the *"new man,"* as St. Paul would say; but this would be better understood psychologically. Our *non-being* is our false self, and our *being* is our real self; and through the natural process of living our life we individuate the consciousness of our *being* and *non-being* and create an immortal, transcendent self—St. Paul's *"new man."* But that's still so abstruse that the only person who would entertain it would be the soul that is so desperate to get out of Plato's cave it would do anything to free itself. A soul like me, for example. I was willing to pay any price to find my true self; but I didn't have an Ariadne's string to find my way out. And that's the story of my life.

PP: *Why don't we take a break and pick this up later?*

OS: Good. I could use a break...

PP: *We were talking about the natural process of soul's individuation through life. Can you explain what you mean by this?*

OS: I've had a long time to work this out, and there's something that I have to say about the self that may help to resolve the paradox of our *being* and *non-being*. We don't have two selves, which everyone seems to think we have; writers like Dostoevsky for example, who wrote *The Double*; Robert Louis Stevenson, who wrote *The Strange Case of Dr. Jekyll and Mr. Hyde*; and Oscar Wilde, who wrote *The Picture of Dorian Gray*. But Goethe put it best in *Faust* when he said that two souls dwell in our breast. If you don't mind, let me Google this just to be sure. Give me a moment, please.

PP: *By all means. It would be nice to see it in context.*

OS: This is from Goethe's play *Faust*:

Two souls alas! are dwelling in my breast;
And each is fain to leave its brother.
The one, fast clinging, to the world adheres
With clutching organs, in love's sturdy lust;
The other strongly lifts itself from dust
To yonder high, ancestral spheres.
Oh, are there spirits hovering near,
That ruling weave, twixt earth and heaven are rife,
Descend! come from the golden atmosphere
And lead me hence to new and varied life!

PP: *I'm familiar with Faust's dilemma, but please continue with what you wanted to say about the self. Again, I sense something almost ominous.*

OS: New insights are ominous because they threaten the status quo. Isn't this what Carl Jung meant by the primitive misoneism of our contemporaries? You're right, what I have to say about the self is almost threatening, because no one has ever put it together this way before. One day I had the startling realization that the "I" of our *being* and the "I" of our *non-being* is the same "I", and depending upon where our "I" is centered determines our sense of reality. Do you see the astounding implications of this realization?

PP: *I do; but your reader may not. Please explain.*

OS: When our "I" is centered in our *being* our reality is different from the reality that we experience when our "I" is centered in our *non-being*, because our *non-being* is not real. The "I" of our *non-being* is our false self, an archetypal karmic matrix of all the unresolved ego-energy of the "I" of our *being*; and the more fixed we are in our *non-being*, the more we see reality falsely—like Macbeth. When I was struggling to extricate myself from the unconscious hold my false self had upon me, Macbeth spoke to my soul. To make my point about our false sense of reality, let me quote Macbeth:

Tomorrow, and tomorrow, and tomorrow,
Creeps in this petty pace from day to day
To the last syllable of recorded time,
And all our yesterdays have lighted fools
The way to dusty death. Out, out, brief candle!
Life's but a walking shadow, a poor player
That struts and frets his hour upon the stage
And then is heard no more. It is a tale
Told by an idiot, full of sound and fury,
Signifying nothing.

PP: *Indeed. This has to be one of Shakespeare's most quoted passages.*
OS: Yes. But what does that tell you?
PP: *That there are a lot of miserable souls out there. So you're saying that when one's "I" is centered in one's non-being one's sense of reality is false, and when one's "I" is centered in their being one's sense of reality is real?*
OS: That's exactly what I'm saying. Life is not a tale told by an idiot full of sound and fury signifying nothing when one is centered in their *being*, because God is the ground of our *being* and we have inherent purpose. We are born to realize our divine nature, and we are driven by the conatus of our spiritual DNA; but not when our "I" is centred in the consciousness of our *non-being*, because this is the consciousness of our nothingness. This is why souls that get stuck in the false self of their *non-being* can be so miserable, like my literary mentor Ernest Hemingway who was so afflicted by his dark shadow self that his third wife Martha Gellhorn called him a pathological liar and cruelest man she knew. That's what inspired my book *The Lion that Swallowed Hemingway*. The lion is Hemingway's shadow. But that's the life

process in action, and not until one learns to resolve the consciousness of their false nature will they be free of their existential anxiety. That was my struggle. But let me quote a poem I wrote that speaks to the soul that gets stuck in the shadow self of their *non-being*, a poem inspired by someone I know, a retired salesman not unlike Willy Loman in Arthur Miller's play *Death of a Salesman*. It will be published in my second book of poetry, which I'm calling *The Devil's Hindquarter:* —

Just Another Angry Man

Have you ever met a man whose
every word fumes with rage, a man
so conflicted that he cannot stand to be
alone and drinks to ease his pain, who
envies anyone who succeeds in life and
finds fault with his wife and children and
politics and religion and everything in
between? He's not the same as you and
and me, this angry man; he seldom laughs
or cracks a smile but snickers like he's
in on some cruel joke that life has played
upon the world, and the more he drinks
the more vicious he becomes, a habit he
cannot break because it's to his nature
to be obstreperous, and he's lonely and
miserable and cannot understand why
the world has turned against him, a
man who would like to change
the way he is but cannot.

    PP: *I've known such men. Let's talk about your struggle, if you don't mind?*

OS: I wouldn't be me if it wasn't for my struggle. But my struggle was different from most people, because mine was a concerted struggle. As I said, I had a sexual experience that catapulted me into my quest for my true self, because I knew that the person who did what he did that night was me but not me, and I vowed to find out who this other me was. That's what set my soul on fire. I had to find out who or what this other me was, and not until Gurdjieff came into my life did I finally make sense of my conflicted nature.

PP: *Life is all about redemption, then?*

OS: Exactly! You do cut to the quick, don't you? Yes, life is all about redeeming ourselves from our false nature. But the problem everyone has is that they can't tell where their center of gravity is—in their *being* or *non-being*. But literature is not enough to resolve the paradox of our *being* and our *non-being*. One has to live the secret way to do that, but not everyone is ready for the secret way; and if they are, it takes more courage than most people have to embrace it. This is the premise of my book *The Merciful Law of Divine Synchronicity*. Life makes us ready for the secret way through karma and reincarnation, and when we have evolved enough life calls us to the secret way. I was called in high school with Maugham's novel *The Razor's Edge*; but one can be called to the monastery, to music, art, poetry, medicine, psychology—whatever. The call to the secret way is individual, as I tried to make clear in my spiritual musings; and by secret way, I mean the spiritual stream of life that flows back home to God. This is not a metaphor. The stream exists; but one has to experience *the living way* to believe it.

PP: *Thank you for that. You've opened up to something I wasn't sure you wanted to talk about, some of the other teachings that you lived; like the solar cult teaching that damaged your eyesight, and the New Age Religion of the Light and Sound of God. Or am I being too presumptuous?*

OS: Give me a moment to think about this, please.

PP: *Certainly. Take all the time you need...*

OS: One of the best tips I got from Ernest Hemingway was to never talk about an experience that I'm going to write about, and I haven't written about my off-shoot Christian solar cult experience yet, nor my experience with the New Age Religion of the Light and Sound of God that I lived for many years. I know now that both of these teachings were necessary for my spiritual growth, but when they had served their purpose *the omniscient guiding principle of life* introduced me to another path to continue my growth which would only have been hampered by these false teachings. Wait. I just remembered. I have a poem in my book that speaks to my experience, which I titled "A New Age Religion." But I still need more distance from this experience before I can write a story about it.

PP: *And what path are you on now, if I may ask?*

OS: I've been called back to creative writing. That's the path I was first called to in my youth before I was called to find my true self with Maugham's novel; that's why I'm concentrating on poetry and short story writing now and my journal/memoir *My Writing Life*, a sequel to *The Lion that Swallowed Hemingway*.

PP: *You've written one book of poetry and are working on another, can you say anything about the short stories you are writing?*

OS: I can talk about one book of stories that I've written. It's called *Sparkles in the Mist and Other Stories*, and it's not unlike Hemingway's Nick Adams stories insomuch that they are no less autobiographical; but not as well-written, I don't think. I have to confess, as much as I learned from Ernest Hemingway, I cannot write like him. His style is too cramped for me. I need the open spaces of the mind, more like John Updike. In fact, the first story in this collection is called "The Genius of Updike." And I've started another book of stories that was inspired by another coincidence when Penny's sister gave me an *Indigo Hemingway Notebook* for Christmas. I've written the first story already, "Hemingway's Forgotten Notebooks," which may become the title of the whole book. It's ironic, but as my life comes to a close

I've come right back to my high school hero and literary mentor Ernest Hemingway. Life never ceases to surprise me. But I wonder where this will lead to?

PP: *On that note, I think we can bring this interview to a close.*

OS: Ironic, isn`t it? Thank you. I enjoyed this very much. And if you don't mind, I think I'm going to include this interview as an addendum to Not My Circus, Not My Monkeys, because it just might be the key to the undiscovered soul of poetry.

ALSO BY OREST STOCCO

NOVELS

The Golden Seed
Tea with Grace
Jesus Wears Dockers
Healing with Padre Pio
Keeper of the Flame
My Unborn Child
On the Wings of Habitat
What Would I Say Today If I Were to Die Tomorrow?

NON-FICTION

The Merciful Law of Divine Synchronicity
Death, the Final Frontier
Gurdjieff Was Wrong, But His Teaching Works
The Man of God Walks Alone
The Summoning of Noman
The Lion that Swallowed Hemingway
The Sum of All Spiritual Paths
Do We Have An Immortal Soul?
Stupidity Is Not a Gift of God
Letters to Padre Pio
Old Whore Life
Just Going with the Flow
Why Bother? The Riddle of the Good Samaritan
The Pearl of Great Price
In The Shade of the Maple Tree

About the Author

Born with a spiritual restlessness that could not be tamed by my Christian faith, I became a spiritual seeker when I discovered reincarnation in Plato's Dialogues at the age of fifteen. I grew up in a small town in Northwestern Ontario, and at twenty-one I had my own pool hall and vending machine business, but my restless spirit called me away to seek out my destiny, and I sold my business and sailed to France.

In the Alpine city of Annecy, in the Haute-Savoie region of France I had a dream that called me to my destiny. I entered into the mind of every person in the world and took every question they had ever asked and reduced them all to one question: *Why am I?* I returned to Canada and went to university to study philosophy to seek an answer to this haunting question, and by "chance" I discovered Gurdjieff, the redoubtable teacher of a system of transformative thought that he called "the Work." His Teaching excited my restless spirit and compelled me to seek out the answer to man's disquieting question in the fast, often tumultuous currents of daily living.

Visit him at: http://ostocco.wix.com/ostocco
Spiritual Musings Blog:
http://www.spiritualmusingsbyoreststocco.blogspot.com

www.ingramcontent.com/pod-product-compliance
Lightning Source LLC
LaVergne TN
LVHW011423080426
835512LV00005B/222